Medieval Tech Today

Do We BATTLE Like It's MEDIEVAL Times?

Military Technology THEN and NOW

by Megan Cooley Peterson

CAPSTONE PRESS
a capstone imprint

Captivate is published by Capstone Press, an imprint of Capstone.
1710 Roe Crest Drive
North Mankato, Minnesota 56003
www.capstonepub.com

Library of Congress Cataloging-in-Publication Data is available on the Library of Congress website.
ISBN: 978-1-4966-8473-8 (hardcover)
ISBN: 978-1-4966-8493-6 (ebook PDF)

Summary:
From gunpowder to armor, medieval innovators helped develop and improve some important weaponry and warfare technology we use today. The Middle Ages were crucial for the development of technologies such as warships, battering rams, cannons, and more! Discover how we still fight like we're in medieval times with interesting historical facts, scientific details, and illuminating art and photos.

Image Credits
Alamy: Atlaspix, 37, Colin Waters, 41, FALKENSTEINFOTO, 35, Ryhor Bruyeu, 13; Getty Images: DEA/C. BALOSSINI, 14; Mary Evans Picture Library: GROSVENOR PRINTS, 17; Newscom: akg-images, 31, Album /British Library, 18, Album /Prisma, 6, 27, 29, 38, Ann Ronan Picture Library Heritage Images, 22, Danita Delimont Photography/Peter Langer, 36, Florilegius/Album, 15, World History Archive, 21; North Wind Picture Archives, 5, 10, 19; Science Source: SHEILA TERRY, 43; Shutterstock: Krunja, 24, Lutsenko_Oleksandr, Cover (Bottom Left); U.S. Army Photo by Staff Sgt. Jennifer Bunn, 2d Cavalry Regiment, 9, Staff Sgt. True Thao, Cover (Bottom Right); U.S. Navy photo by Mass Communication Specialist 3rd Class Kody A. Phillips, 33; Wikimedia: Fotograf Walter Frentz, 26

The appearance of U.S. Department of Defense (DoD) visual information does not imply or constitute DoD endorsement.

Design Elements
Capstone; Shutterstock: andromina, Curly Pat, derGriza, Evgeniya Mokeeva, Kompaniets Taras, lightmood, ONYXprj, Tartila, yalcinart

Editorial Credits
Editor: Eliza Leahy; Designer: Sarah Bennett; Media Researcher: Jo Miller; Production Specialist: Katy LaVigne

All internet sites appearing in back matter were available and accurate when this book was sent to press.

Printed and bound in the United States of America.
PA117

Table of Contents

Words in **bold** are in the glossary.

CHAPTER 1

War in the Middle Ages

A knight rides his horse onto a battlefield. Lances meet. Men yell. The knight's muscles strain as he carries the weight of his metal armor. He raises his sword and slashes at an enemy soldier. Then he spins his horse around to face the next enemy. Blood spills into the dirt. He has no time to rest.

Medieval warfare was dangerous. Soldiers didn't have jet fighters or computerized weapons. They fought in hand-to-hand combat. Each step onto the battlefield could be a soldier's last. Many weapons were invented or developed during the Middle Ages. Gunpowder and cannons made warfare even more deadly. Warships brought fighting to the sea. The Middle Ages changed the way wars were fought.

French knights fought against English soldiers during the Hundred Years' War (1337–1453).

The Middle Ages

There were three periods of the Middle Ages: Early Middle Ages, High Middle Ages, and Late Middle Ages. This was also referred to as the medieval times. The Middle Ages was from the late 400s to AD 1500.

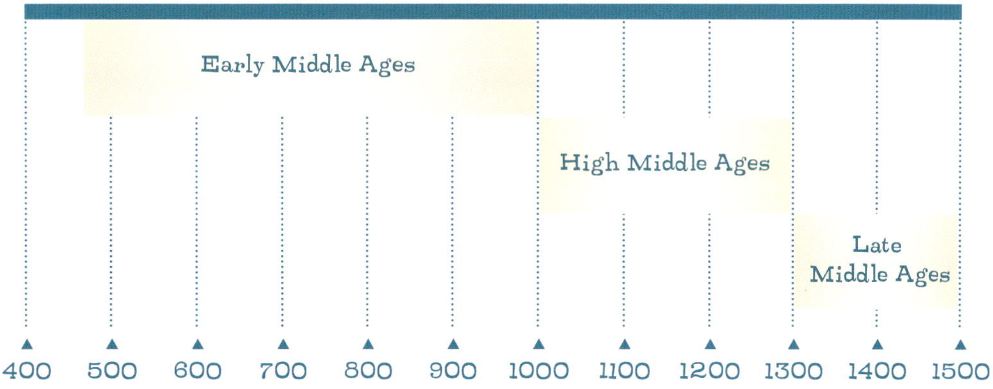

The Middle Ages began in AD 476 with the fall of the Western Roman Empire. Many European tribes battled for land and power. A group called the Ostrogoths settled in Italy, Greece, and the western Balkans. The Franks took over France, Belgium, and western Germany. The Saxons conquered most of England. The Visigoths seized Spain, and the Vandals moved into North Africa.

Roderic was the last Visigothic king of Spain. He died in battle in AD 711.

Throughout the Middle Ages, most of the land in Europe was divided into kingdoms. Since a king couldn't watch over all his land, he handed it out to trusted nobles. The nobles further divided their land among lords, who were required to fight as knights at the king's request. Successful knights were rewarded with land and riches. Kingdoms rose and fell. Land changed hands after bloody battles.

Hierarchy of the Middle Ages

king: The king was the top ruler of the land. The king chose nobles to watch over his land.

noble: The king gave noblemen large pieces of land, called fiefs. Each noble broke up his fief into smaller pieces, called manors. These were held by lesser nobles. In return for their lands, nobles gave the king loyalty. Nobles often served as leaders of the king's army, when required.

peasant: The peasant was the lowest class. Many peasants were farmers. Peasants could become blacksmiths, bakers, or other workers. They paid rent to the lords.

CHAPTER 2

Armor

Today's soldiers do everything they can to protect themselves during combat. They wear heavy boots and helmets. Shirts have elbow pads built in, and pants have knee pads. Some helmets wrap around the lower half of the face. Many armies have developed **exoskeleton** armor. This armor has Kevlar plates to block bullets and flying debris. Kevlar is a strong, heat-resistant plastic that's bulletproof. It's also five times stronger than steel. Motorized joints in the knees and elbows help soldiers move more easily.

The U.S. Army is also developing a liquid armor. Kevlar is soaked in a special type of fluid. The fluid is called a shear thickening fluid. If a bullet hits the vest, the fluid instantly becomes very hard. Soldiers will be able to move more easily on the battlefield in this lightweight armor.

U.S. soldiers wear heavy boots, helmets, and other items to protect themselves in combat.

Medieval knights wore chain mail, which is made from thousands of metal rings bound together.

Soldiers and knights in the Middle Ages also wore armor, from chain mail to metal plate armor. The armor had to be strong enough to protect them from a sword's or arrow's blow. It also had to be flexible enough for the soldier to move in.

Early Medieval Armor

After the fall of Rome, European tribes fought for territory. They waged war almost constantly in the early Middle Ages. Most soldiers wore armor, usually passed down to them. Even something as simple as leather, wool, or furs could be worn as armor. They carried shields made of wood ringed with metal and sometimes covered with leather. Nobles wore helmets and body armor. These metal helmets had pieces protecting the cheeks. Many soldiers also relied on chain mail for protection.

FACT

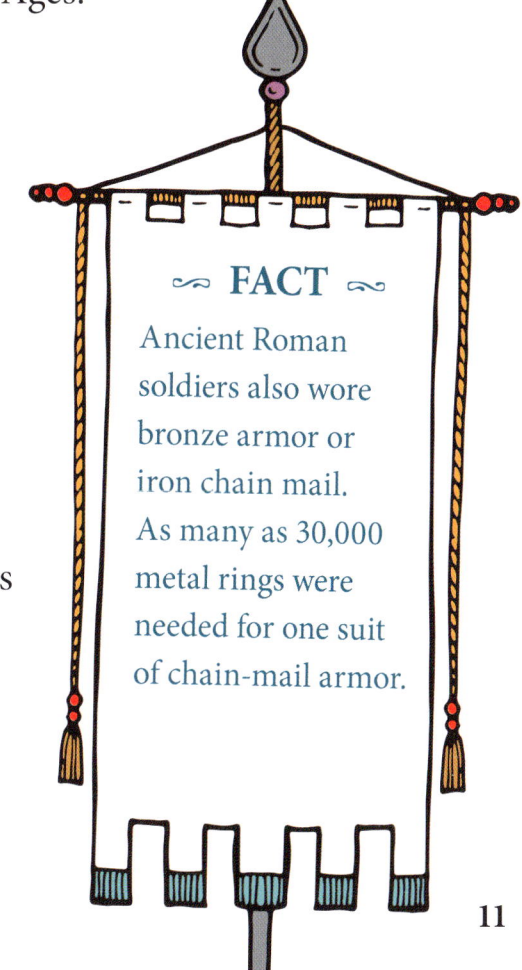

Ancient Roman soldiers also wore bronze armor or iron chain mail. As many as 30,000 metal rings were needed for one suit of chain-mail armor.

Plate Armor

By the 1300s, a new type of body armor had developed—plate armor. At first, plates were added only to the knee and elbow joints. These plates were made of iron or bronze. Plate armor covering the shins was also invented around this same time.

By the mid-1400s, some medieval knights wore full-body plate armor into battle. This was the most expensive type of armor. Only the wealthiest soldiers could afford it. Skilled metalworkers, called armorers, made each steel plate by hand. The plates had to fit together like a puzzle. Each plate was thinner at the edges. This allowed better movement for the knight. Knights wore a tight-fitting jacket underneath the plates. The jacket protected their skin from the metal.

Medieval military armor on display at a museum inside the Tower of Kamyenyets in Belarus

Plate armor fell out of style by 1650. With the invention of gunpowder weapons, soldiers fought in less hand-to-hand combat. Over time, opposing soldiers began fighting more at a distance. The days of plate armor and mounted knights were over.

FACT

Many medieval soldiers wore **gambesons.** Gambesons were padded felt or leather worn under their armor.

Horse Armor

A skilled knight needed a strong horse to ride into battle. The horse gave a knight extra power and speed. In the early 1200s, knights began equipping their horses with armor. Horses wore padding and chain mail on their sides to protect from arrows and sword blows. By the 1300s, wealthy knights added pieces of metal plate armor to their horse's armor.

CHAPTER 3

The Longbow

In 2010, archer Randy Oitker stood under the hot studio lights of *Jimmy Kimmel Live*. Holding his compound bow, he faced a target with seven balloons attached. His goal was to pop all seven balloons in a single shot. As the audience watched, Oitker loaded seven arrows into his bow all at once. He pulled them back and shot. But the arrows he shot only popped six balloons. Oitker missed one on his second try too. He had one final shot to take. The arrows flew toward their target, hitting all seven balloons. Oitker had just set the world record, breaking his previous record of six balloons in one shot.

Today, hunters and archers rely on the compound bow for its speed and accuracy. Compound bows are made from lightweight materials, such as aluminum. A series of cables and **pulleys** bend the bow.

During the late Middle Ages, English soldiers used the longbow to shoot arrows into enemy lines. The longbow was much simpler than the modern compound bow. A medieval longbow was made of a single length of wood, usually from an ash or yew tree. The bowstring was made from linen and hemp. These fibers were woven together to create a strong string. The arrows had wooden shafts tipped with iron or steel heads. The heads could dent plate armor and chain mail. But they could not pierce them.

FACT

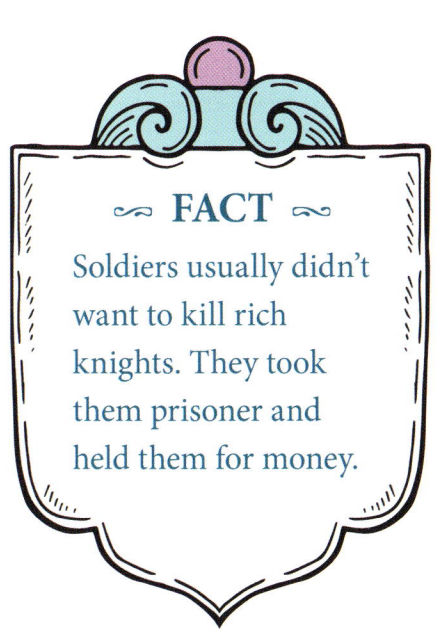

Soldiers usually didn't want to kill rich knights. They took them prisoner and held them for money.

The Longbow in Battle

In battle, medieval archers likely flanked the main troops. To shoot, they pulled the arrow all the way back to their ear before letting go. The English longbow had a range of about 200 feet (60 meters). Archers probably didn't kill a lot of enemy soldiers, but they did injure them. An injured soldier couldn't fight as effectively, which was the archer's goal.

Medieval archers shot at a castle during battle as soldiers scaled the walls.

FACT

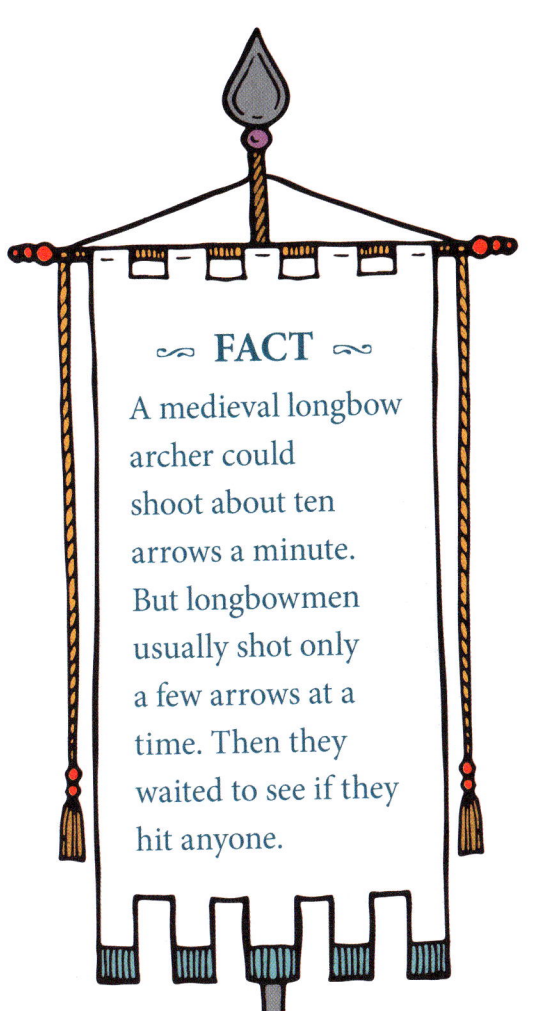

A medieval longbow archer could shoot about ten arrows a minute. But longbowmen usually shot only a few arrows at a time. Then they waited to see if they hit anyone.

The longbow was an important weapon used by the English during the Hundred Years' War. This war between England and France began in 1337. France's King Charles IV had no heirs when he died. His nephew King Edward III of England believed he should inherit the French throne. French nobles disagreed. They supported King Philip VI, a cousin of Charles IV.

The Crossbow

The crossbow was widely used by European armies in the Middle Ages. The crossbow had a shorter bow than the longbow. The crossbow was also stronger. The arrow was pulled back and then locked into place. Archers pulled a firing trigger to shoot the arrow.

CHAPTER 4

The Battering Ram

In July 2019, engineer Jason Levin flew a drone into the air about 100 feet (30 m). He let the drone hover. Then he used his computer to launch a second drone—one he had built, nicknamed Interceptor. This drone had a battering ram about the size of a lunchbox attached to its top. Levin flew Interceptor underneath the first drone. Then he typed in the command to attack. Interceptor shot up at 100 miles (160 kilometers) per hour. It bashed the first drone out of the air.

Militaries around the world use drones to monitor and attack enemies. But they couldn't knock enemy drones out of the sky until Levin built his battering-ram drone.

The battering ram has been used in combat since ancient times. Assyrian warriors used battering rams as early as the ninth century BC. Wall carvings show battering rams mounted on wheels. Soldiers covered battering rams with wicker mats and made them look like animals. The mats were soaked with water to prevent them from catching fire.

A carving of an Assyrian four-wheeled battering ram during battle

Medieval Battering Rams

In the Middle Ages, the battering ram was an important part of **siege** warfare. During a siege, a medieval army would surround an enemy city or castle. Many cities and castles were protected by strong stone walls. The wall's gate was usually made from wood. It was the wall's weakest point. Armies would break down the gate, storm into the city, and attack the enemy. And they used battering rams to do it.

Soldiers used a battering ram to break through a castle wall.

The first battering rams used in medieval warfare were likely made of large tree trunks. The tree trunks were hung from ropes or chains attached to a structure. The tree trunk was pulled back like a swing and then released. It could also be carried by soldiers and rammed into the target. Attacking soldiers used catapults to sweep enemy soldiers off the walls.

In some cases, defenders caught the battering ram with hooks or ropes. Then they pulled it over the wall. Archers also shot arrows down at the attacking soldiers who were running the battering ram. Sometimes soldiers dropped heavy stones or pots of fire onto the battering rams. Later, soldiers added roofs to their battering rams to protect them.

FACT

Medieval soldiers also used ladders to climb enemy walls. Siege towers were built around ladders to protect the climbing soldiers. Battering rams were built into the bottom level of a siege tower.

CHAPTER 5

Gunpowder

Around the world, people enjoy colorful fireworks displays to celebrate everything from Halloween to New Year's Eve. To celebrate New Year's Day in 2016, the Church of Christ in the Philippines put on the largest fireworks show in history. The show began as soon as the clock struck midnight. For the next hour, spectators watched as 810,904 individual fireworks exploded in the night sky.

What gives fireworks their boom? Gunpowder. The Chinese invented gunpowder, also called black powder, in the mid-800s. Gunpowder is made by mixing sulfur, charcoal, and saltpeter. When ignited, this powder burns quickly. When the powder is burned in a confined space, it can cause an explosion.

Gunpowder arrived in Europe by the mid-1200s. Some historians believe **missionaries** may have brought gunpowder to Europe from Asia. Gunpowder led to the creation of new types of weapons, from cannons to handguns. Warfare in the Middle Ages was about to change.

FACT

Black gunpowder makes a lot of smoke when fired. Most guns today use smokeless powder.

CHAPTER 6

Cannons

In 2019, the U.S. Army announced it was working on a new cannon to be used on the ground. The Strategic Long Range Cannon has a range of more than 1,000 miles (1,600 km). Troops can launch long-distance attacks with this super cannon. The idea of a super-sized cannon isn't new. During World War II, the Germans designed a huge cannon called the Gustav. It had a range of 29 miles (47 km). This cannon weighed around 1,300 tons. Soldiers today use powerful computers to aim and fire cannons.

The Gustav had to be transported by railway.

Armies in the Middle Ages also used cannons and gunpowder in battle. No one is quite sure when the first cannons were used in medieval Europe. Two illustrations made in London in 1326 show a cannon shaped like a vase lying on its side. A soldier is holding a hot iron to the cannon. The cannon appears to be made of bronze. These are two of the first-known records of cannons used in the Middle Ages.

The Trebuchet

Before the cannon, many medieval armies used **trebuchets** during sieges. This catapult weapon was powered by human muscle instead of gunpowder. It could fling 400-pound (136-kilogram) stones at enemy walls. And they could throw them up to 900 feet (274 m). Soldiers even launched dead animals into enemy cities, hoping to spread disease.

Most medieval cannons were made of bronze or wrought iron. To make the barrel of the cannon, long strips of metal were laid edge to edge. Then rings of metal were placed over the barrel to hold the strips together. The rings were slightly smaller in diameter than the barrel. To make them fit, the rings were heated until they expanded. Then they were slipped onto the barrel. As the rings cooled, they shrunk down, holding the barrel together tightly.

FACT

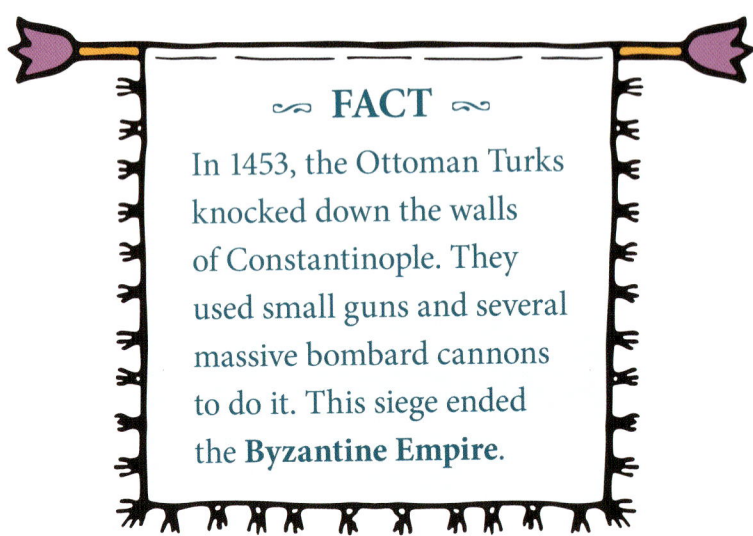

In 1453, the Ottoman Turks knocked down the walls of Constantinople. They used small guns and several massive bombard cannons to do it. This siege ended the **Byzantine Empire**.

The Bombard

The bombard was the largest cannon used in medieval warfare. A bombard could weigh as much as 22 tons. (Most cars today only weigh around 2 tons.) Medieval soldiers moved bombards on strong carts. Once at the battle, the soldiers used cranes to lift them onto wooden frames. They also used cranes to load them with gunpowder and balls. Wooden walls were then set up around the bombard to protect the soldiers firing it.

Medieval bombards could measure up to 17 feet (5.2 m) long.

Cannons in Battle

By about 1375, historical records included more references to cannons used during siege warfare. In 1377, the French Duke of Burgundy attacked Odruik Castle near the town of Calais in France. The English occupied the castle. During the siege, soldiers used cannons to fire about 200 large bolts at the castle walls. The walls held, but those defending the castle surrendered.

The siege of Maastricht in the Netherlands lasted from November 1407 to January 1408. The town was hit by more than 1,500 large sandstone and limestone balls. But the town did not fall.

By the 1400s, cannons were also used on the battlefields with more frequency. But they were usually inaccurate and didn't affect the battle's outcome.

Medieval cannons fired heavy stones and metal balls.

CHAPTER 7

Warships

The U.S. Navy's Nimitz-Class aircraft carrier looks like a city floating on the water. The largest warship in the world, it measures 1,092 feet (333 m) long and 23 stories tall. Two nuclear reactors power this ship. It can run for 20 years before needing to be refueled!

Around 5,000 crewmembers live and work on this giant ship. The flight deck is 4.5 acres, about the same size as three football fields. With four on-deck catapults, one aircraft can be launched every 20 seconds. As the aircraft races down the short runway, the catapult launches it into the air. The Navy relies on its aircraft carriers to protect its troops around the world.

Modern warships are impressive machines, but they had very simple beginnings. The world's first ships were used for carrying goods and people, not for war. Historians aren't sure when the first warships were used.

The Nimitz-Class aircraft carrier USS *Dwight D. Eisenhower*

An ancient Greek vase from 1400 BC shows what looks like a warship. This might be the first-known record of a warship.

In the early Middle Ages, Western European tribes mainly battled each other on land. They used many types of ships, including cargo ships, to transport soldiers. It is unlikely that these ships were built or used for war. Many coastal kingdoms were caught off guard by a rising shipbuilding power—the Vikings.

Viking Warships

The Vikings were some of the most-feared warriors of the Middle Ages. They lived in modern-day Norway, Sweden, and Denmark. Most Vikings were peaceful farmers, but some set sail to **raid** other lands. In the early 700s, Vikings began building longships with strong **keels**. A keel is the bottom structure of a ship. It runs the length of the ship. The **hull** is built around it.

FACT

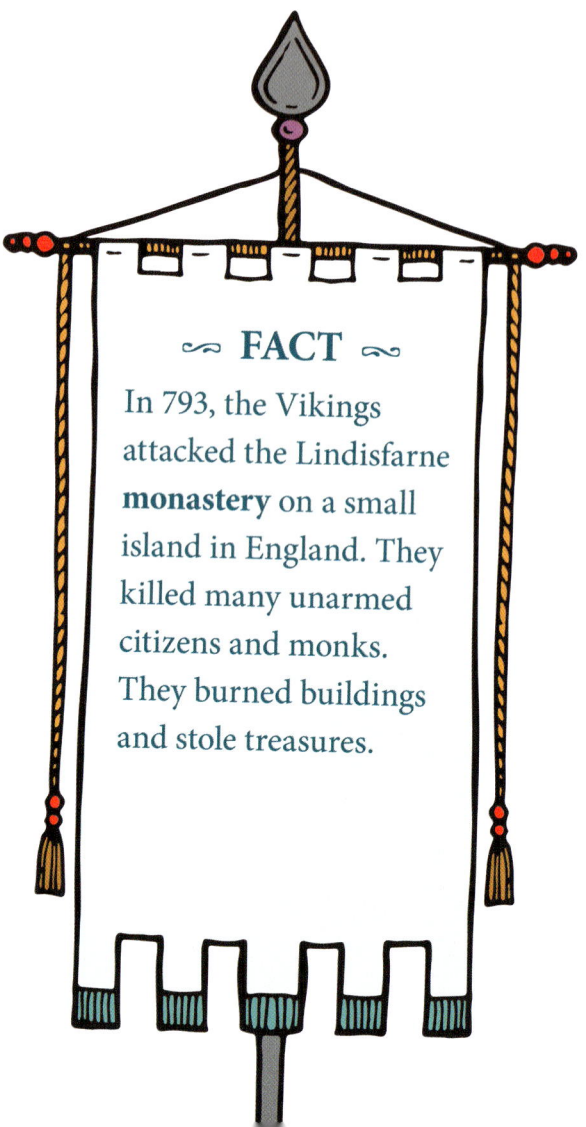

In 793, the Vikings attacked the Lindisfarne **monastery** on a small island in England. They killed many unarmed citizens and monks. They burned buildings and stole treasures.

Viking shipbuilders were able to create deeper and longer ships that could carry heavy masts. These strong ships were able to sail across rough ocean waters and along rivers.

Viking longships invaded England around AD 900.

Viking ships varied in size. A Viking ship was found in a burial mound at Gokstad, Norway, in 1879. The ship was 75 feet (23 m) long and 17 feet (5.2 m) wide. In 1962, several Viking ships were uncovered at Skuldelev, Denmark, including a longship. This ship was 98 feet (30 m) long and 12 feet (3.8 m) wide. Historians believe 65 to 75 men used oars to power this longship.

Viking warriors usually attacked on land. But they did fight in a few battles at sea. In 1000, the Battle of Svolder was fought in the Baltic Sea.

A Viking ship found in a burial mound is on display at the Viking Ship Museum in Oslo, Norway.

Norway's King Olaf Tryggvason and his fleet met the kings of Denmark and Sweden. King Olaf's fleet was large and included the longships *Long Serpent*, *Short Serpent*, and *Crane*. But his fleet had never fought a battle at sea. The Danish and Swedish fleets closed in, trapping Olaf's ships. The bloody battle ended with King Olaf jumping overboard and drowning.

During the Battle of Svolder, warriors fought on the ships' decks with swords and bows.

Warships During the Crusades

The first **Crusade** began in 1095. Christians in Western Europe wanted to take control of lands that they considered holy. These first Crusaders traveled by land. Later, Italian fleets transported men and supplies in smaller ships called coasters. These ships kept close to the coastline. They were not built for warfare or the open sea.

French knights traveled by sea during the first Crusade.

Larger two-masted ships called nefs could sail directly across the Mediterranean Sea to the holy lands. By the late 1100s, crossbowmen also stood on the decks, ready to fight at a moment's notice. Still, naval battles were rare during the Crusades.

Battles at Sea

Battles at sea became more common in the 1200s. European kingdoms fought one another for control of land and trade routes. Coastal Italian cities such as Genoa and Venice greatly increased their fleets, which became the strongest in the region. They fought many naval battles against each other into the 1400s. Some historians say these open-water battles marked the beginning of modern naval warfare.

FACT

In 1225, the Venetian navy required soldiers to carry a broad sword, a dagger, lances, a helmet, and a shield.

CHAPTER 8

Chemical Weapons

Armies throughout history have used whatever weapons they could to defeat their enemies, including chemical weapons. Chemical weapons are gases or other substances that can kill large groups of people quickly, and often painfully. During World War I (1914-1918), several countries used chemical weapons, such as mustard gas. By the end of the war, as many as 100,000 people had died from chemical attacks.

In 1925, many countries came together to ban the use of chemical weapons in future wars. Still, the use of chemical weapons didn't end. Some governments even used these weapons against civilians. Finally, in 1993, many countries signed the Chemical Weapons Convention treaty. This banned the production and use of chemical weapons. These countries also agreed to destroy any stockpiles of these weapons. Sadly, some countries today still use chemical weapons. Armies during the Middle Ages also used chemical weapons. Though dangerous, medieval chemical weapons were not as devastating as modern ones.

British soldiers wore gas masks to protect themselves from chemical attacks during World War I.

Quicklime

Medieval soldiers fighting at close range sometimes attacked each other with quicklime. Quicklime was made by heating limestone to a very high temperature. Then it was ground into a powder. During an attack, soldiers poured quicklime onto their enemies. The soldiers choked on the powder. This powder could also momentarily blind them.

Greek Fire

In the early Middle Ages, a mysterious chemical weapon was developed in the Byzantine Empire. Called Greek fire, historians today still aren't quite sure what it was. Early Greek fire was probably a liquid that could catch fire. It was sprayed from a nozzle. Later, Greek fire was put into small ceramic grenades. Greek fire may have burned even on the water's surface.

The Bloody Middle Ages

Warfare during the Middle Ages was not for the faint of heart. Soldiers fought in bloody battles for their lords and kings. As medieval kingdoms grew, new weapons were developed and invented for battle.

Medieval soldiers used a trebuchet to launch Greek fire over the castle wall.

Knights in plate armor rode bravely into battle. Armies attacked castles and walled cities with battering rams and cannons. Navies took the fighting to the sea on warships. Many modern armies use weapons whose origins can be traced back to medieval times.

Timeline of Technology

AD 671–678
Byzantine ships are fitted with Greek fire to defend the city of Constantinople.

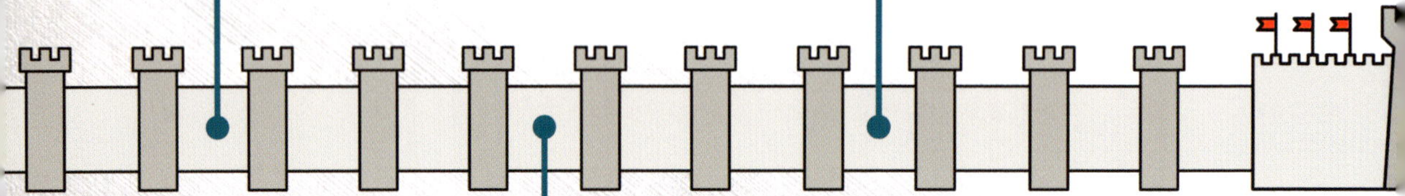

AD 711
The Anglo-Saxons invading England have battering rams.

late 700s
Viking warriors begin attacking lands in Europe. They sail across the sea in longships.

AD 885
The Vikings attack Paris with a siege tower.

around the 1300s
A type of Greek fire is used by Europeans.

1326
An illustration shows a medieval soldier firing a cannon. This illustration is one of the first-known records of cannons being used in the Middle Ages.

1337–1453
The Hundred Years' War is fought between the kingdoms of England and France.

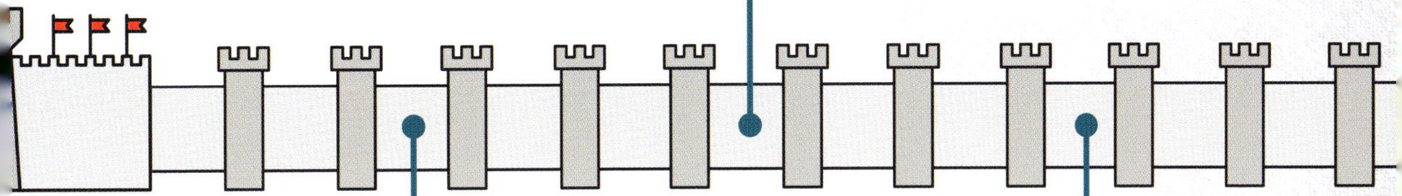

mid-1200s
Gunpowder first arrives in Europe from Asia.

1450
Knights begin wearing full plate armor into battle.

1453
The Ottoman Turks knock down the walls of Constantinople using large cannons called bombards.

Glossary

Byzantine Empire (BIZ-uhn-teen EM-pire)—a civilization that spread throughout eastern Europe and northern Africa during the Middle Ages

Crusades (kroo-SAYDZ)—battles fought between AD 1000 and 1300 by European Christians trying to capture Biblical lands from non-Christians

exoskeleton (ek-soh-SKE-luh-tuhn)—a structure on the outside of modern armor that gives it support

hull (HUHL)— the frame or body of a ship or aircraft

keel (KEEL)—the wooden or metal piece that runs along the bottom of a boat

missionary (MISH-uh-nair-ee)—a person who works on behalf of a religious group to spread the group's faith

monastery (MAH-nuh-ster-ee)—a group of buildings where monks live and work

pulley (PUL-ee)—a grooved wheel turned by a rope, belt, or chain that often moves heavy objects

raid (RAYD)—a sudden, surprise attack on a place

siege (SEEJ)—an attack designed to surround a place and cut it off from supplies or help

trebuchet (tre-byoo-SHET)—a medieval war machine used to throw heavy rocks

Read More

Bow, James. *Your Guide to Castles and Medieval Warfare*. New York: Crabtree Publishing Company, 2017.

Lassieur, Allison. *Medieval Knight Science: Armor, Weapons, and Siege Warfare*. North Mankato, MN: Capstone Press, 2017.

Roesser, Marie. *The Middle Ages*. New York: Gareth Stevens Publishing, 2020.

Internet Sites

Medieval Arms Race
https://www.pbs.org/wgbh/nova/lostempires/trebuchet/race.html

Middle Ages
https://www.history.com/topics/middle-ages

The Middle Ages
https://www.bl.uk/the-middle-ages

Select Bibliography

Newman, Paul B. *Daily Life in the Middle Ages*. London: McFarland and Co., 2001.

Index